Star Struck

Debbie White

Illustrated by Tony Ross

OXF
UNIVERS

D1513561

1
Harrison gives it a go

'No way,' said Harrison.

'Please. Just for me.'

'No,' said Harrison. 'Violins are boring. I want to play the saxophone, like Carl.'

'Mmn,' said Harrison's mum, slamming a plate of sandwiches down on the table. 'We'll see about that.'

'Saxophones are really great, Mrs Bellringer,' said Carl. 'They're dead easy to play.'

'They cost a lot too. I can't afford it at the moment. The car needs mending. Anyway, playing the violin's in the family. Your great grandmother was a child prodigy, Harrison. She was playing Beethoven when she was six.'

'Beethoven?' said Harrison, looking blank.

'He wrote wonderful music,' said Mrs Bellringer with a sigh.

'And what's a child prodigy?' asked Carl.

'Someone who does something really well, when they're very young,' she explained.

'Like a ten-year-old boy playing football in the World Cup?' said Carl. 'They'd be really famous if they did that. They'd make loads of money *and* be on the telly.'

Harrison liked the sound of that.

'If I was a child prodigy, would I be a star?'

'Of course you would,' said Mrs Bellringer.

'OK,' said Harrison. 'I'll give it a go and when I'm famous, you can have a new car.'

2
Something in the attic

So, quick as a flash, Harrison was having violin lessons at school. His teacher was Mr Batz, who had big, black bags under his eyes and a double chin that wobbled.

No more Tuesday lunchtimes playing football with his mates.

Even worse, Harrison had to share his lessons with a girl called Emily Snell. She loved playing the violin and did loads of practice.

When Emily played, Mr Batz said,
'*Bravissima!*' (really great) and smiled
a lot.

When Harrison scraped his bow across
the strings, it sounded like two cats
fighting.

Poor Harrison. He was very fed up.
He'd set his heart on being a star.

Then suddenly, one Tuesday, everything changed.

Harrison was halfway through playing *Twinkle, Twinkle*, when Mr Batz shouted, 'Stop! Harrison, these violin lessons are a waste of time. You have the musical talent of a small gnat. Please ask your mother to come and see me as soon as possible.'

Emily Snell smirked. She was looking forward to having lessons on her own in future.

Oh well, thought Harrison. He wasn't that bothered. He was useless at playing the violin *and* he missed playing football with his mates. Mum would understand.

But on the way home in the car, Harrison started to worry. Would his mum let him give up the violin?

'Flaming Nora,' said Mrs Bellringer, as they lurched down the road. 'This car's a total wreck. It'll cost a fortune to repair.'

'Don't worry,' said Harrison quickly. 'I'll give up my violin lessons. That'll save loads of money, won't it?'

'No,' said Mrs Bellringer. 'You have star quality. I won't let you give up.'

Harrison was amazed. His mum listened to him practise every night after tea. Star quality? Now that would take a miracle.

Harrison had a little think. How could he make his mum change her mind?

Then he said, 'Mr Batz says I need a new violin. He says my school one's rubbish.'

'Did he?' said Mrs Bellringer. 'How much will that cost?'

'Hundreds,' said Harrison slyly. 'Thousands even.'

Mrs Bellringer looked horrified. She hadn't got hundreds of pounds, let alone thousands.

But then, all of a sudden she cried, 'What a ding-bat I am! Your great grandmother had a wonderful violin. I bet it's still in the attic somewhere.'

'Did you ever play it, Mum?' asked Harrison, suddenly curious.

'Oooh no,' said Mrs Bellringer. 'Your great grandma wouldn't let anyone near it. I learnt the piano instead, but I wasn't any good. "Sylvia," my teacher used to say, "you have the musical talent of a small gnat." Thank goodness you don't take after me.'

When they got home, Mrs Bellringer wanted to rush straight up to the attic.

'But Carl's coming round in five minutes,' said Harrison. 'We're doing a project together on Egyptian mummies.'

'All right, but I can't wait to hear you play. You'll sound even better on a good violin.'

Harrison and Carl held the ladder,
while Mrs Bellringer climbed into
the attic.

Bang. Crash. Ouch.

'It's very dark up here,' she shouted.

Cough. Splutter. Sneeze.

'And very dusty.'

'Come down then,' Harrison called
out hopefully.

'I'll just look … Yes! Here it is. Now
grab hold, I'm passing it down.'

'Come on, Harrison. Open it up,' said Mrs Bellringer, once they were downstairs. She was very excited.

Harrison looked at the black case, lying on the kitchen table. He felt worried, just like he did when they had a maths test at school.

'Yes, go on,' said Carl. 'Quick.'

Harrison turned the silver key in the lock.

He lifted the lid. There, wrapped in a blue silk scarf, was his great grandmother's violin.

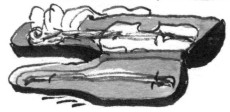

'Take it out,' said Mrs Bellringer. 'Play
us something nice.'

'He can't,' said Carl. He'd heard
Harrison play once before.

'Rubbish,' said Mrs Bellringer. 'Just get
on with it.'

3

Proper, grown-up music

Harrison picked up the violin. He carefully tucked it under his chin. He drew the bow across the strings and started to play. Real, proper, grown-up music.

For a minute he couldn't believe what he was hearing. Then he closed his eyes – carried away by the wonderful sound.

Carl's mouth dropped open. His eyes nearly popped out of his head.

'Wow!' he said. 'That's what I call playing!'

'Well,' said Mrs Bellringer, 'I thought you played that Beethoven beautifully.'

Poor Harrison. He was in shock. He couldn't speak. Never mind, Mrs Bellringer was talking for two.

But all Harrison could think about was the violin. How it had nestled between his chin and shoulder. How the bow had flowed across the strings and made them sing. Mr Batz was going to get a big surprise on Tuesday. So was Emily Snell. Harrison grinned. All of a sudden, he was feeling quite cheerful.

'But you mustn't let it go to your head,' Mrs Bellringer said sharply. 'You're still just a boy. What you need is plenty of rest. So Carl, jump in the car. I'm taking you home. Harrison, into bed double-quick.'

For once, Harrison did as he was told. There would be time to try out his school violin before his mum came back. Maybe he could play Beethoven on his school violin too?

He tucked it under his chin and he started to play.

Screech, whine, yowl. Oh, no. It still sounded like two cats fighting.

Then he picked up his great grandmother's violin. Goodness me, what a wonderful sound!

'Help!' he said, quickly pushing the violin as far under the bed as it would go. He knew it was there though. Waiting.

No one could make him play, could they? But he knew that, really, he wanted to. It made him feel excited. He'd be a star. People would take notice.

4

Harrison, a star?

'I never knew you could play like that,'
said Carl admiringly, the next morning.
He'd been waiting for Harrison at the
school gates. 'Last time I heard you
practise, you were awful.'

'It's not me playing,' said Harrison,
looking miserable.

'Eh?' said Carl.

'It's the violin,' said Harrison. 'It just
sort of takes over.'

'Spooky,' said Carl.

'I couldn't sleep last night just
thinking about it. And Mum's been
going mad this morning. Telephoning
the local paper and everything. She's
told them to meet us at school this
lunchtime.'

'Why?' asked Carl.

'To hear me play,' said Harrison,
looking pale.

'Phew!' said Carl.

Harrison nodded.

'What am I going to do?'

'Tell your mum you don't want to play. Tell her you hate the violin. Tell her you'd rather play football.'

'Huh!' said Harrison. 'She won't take any notice.'

Carl shook his head. Harrison was right. Mrs Bellringer wasn't very good at listening.

Harrison looked glum.

'So I expect I'll end up doing what she wants. Anyway,' he said, cheering up a bit, 'being a child star might be fun. I bet you get loads of time off school.'

'But you wouldn't be a proper one. You'd get found out,' said Carl. 'Then you'd be in worse trouble.'

'No, I wouldn't,' said Harrison. 'You're just being a wimp.'

'I'm not a wimp,' said Carl furiously, and he stomped off, leaving Harrison on his own in the playground.

By lunchtime, Harrison was missing
his friend badly.

The small hall where Harrison had his
violin lessons had been taken over by
the Press.

'Tell us what it's like to teach a child
star, Mr Batz,' demanded a reporter.

'Well,' said Mr Batz, thinking they
must be talking about Emily, 'Miss Snell
is certainly very talented, but ...'

'Not her,' shouted another reporter impatiently. 'It's Harrison Bellringer we've come to hear.'

Poor Mr Batz. Was this some kind of horrible joke? Harrison Bellringer, a star?

'Come on, Harrison, play us something nice,' said a woman from the TV.

Oh dear, what should he do? Play Beethoven on his great grandmother's violin, or *Twinkle, Twinkle* on his school one?

Did he want to be a star, or just plain Harrison Bellringer, playing football with his mates?

For a nano-second he wavered. His hand hovered between the two violins.

Just as he was about to choose, there was a big kerfuffle at the back of the hall. There was a buzz of voices as a little old lady, dressed all in black, elbowed her way to the front.

'Boy,' she commanded, 'leave that violin alone.'

Harrison froze.

5

Madame Mara gets a grip

'Excuse me!' said Mrs Bellringer,
stepping forward.

'Excuse me!' said Mr Batz.

'Who are you?' demanded the woman
in black.

'I'm his mother.'

'I'm his teacher.'

'And I,' she said, 'am the great
Madame Viola D'Amore.'

'Not the famous violinist, *Zara* Viola
D'Amore?' said Mr Batz.

'My dear young man,' she said – and she was talking to Mr Batz! – 'Do I look dead? ... No, I am her daughter, *Mara* Viola D'Amore – the great violin teacher.'

She turned to the sea of reporters behind her. 'Now, I need to speak with my new pupil, Harrison. Come back at seven tonight when you will hear marvellous things.'

There was a pause. Then a sudden rush as all the reporters tried to squeeze out of the hall together. Harrison could see them out in the playground, making frantic calls on their mobile phones.

Perhaps I'll just nip out and find Carl, thought Harrison. No one will notice.

No such luck. He was cornered. Madame Mara had him quickly in her grip.

'What's all this about Harrison being your pupil?' demanded Mrs Bellringer.

'Say nothing,' said Madame Mara. 'I am a great violin teacher. My lessons are very expensive. But, for Harrison, I charge nothing. I can't wait to get my hands on him.'

And the violin, thought Harrison. Somehow, she knows it's special.

'Come, Harrison,' said Madame Mara sweetly. 'Give me your violin.'

Harrison picked up his school one.

'Not that thing,' she snapped. Her hand reached out, but Harrison was there first. He snatched up his great grandmother's violin and started to run.

He made it out of the school and then out of the playground.

Help! He'd forgotten about the pack of reporters.

Oh, no! They'd spotted him. Luckily, so had Carl.

'I'll head 'em off. Meet me in the library,' Carl shouted.

Harrison nodded.

Then the pack was closing in and he made his escape – out of the school gates, down the hill and round the corner to the library.

Harrison stopped. He'd be safe in the library. No reporter was going to get past Mrs Pauley, head librarian and Book Beast.

Bang. Slam. Crash. The way she checked out books was terrifying.

Harrison sidled into the library, violin tucked under his arm. Mrs Pauley turned round suddenly.

'Harrison Bellringer! Why aren't you in school?'

'Er,' said Harrison, thinking fast. 'Mr Batz sent me to find out about violins. See, look at this.'

He pushed the violin under her nose. She took it. Then she held it up under the light and peered in through the sound holes.

'Sometimes,' she said, 'they have the maker's name inside. Yes! There it is: *Alfredo Romeo, Cremona, Italy*. Let's key his name into the computer and see what comes up.'

6

A spell of trouble

Harrison was sitting quietly in a corner of the library. He was looking at the computer print-out Mrs Pauley had given him, when Carl appeared.

Carl looked pleased with himself.

'I bet you want to know how I gave them the slip?' he said.

'Not now,' said Harrison. 'Just read this. It's all about the violin.'

Carl looked horrified. He hated
reading.

'Oh all right,' said Harrison. 'I'll just
explain instead. A long time ago in Italy,
there was a great gypsy violin maker. His
name was Alfredo Romeo, but everyone
called him Fred.'

Carl nodded, so Harrison continued.

'Fred couldn't play the violin for
toffee, but the ones he made were
brilliant. And the more he made, the
better they got.'

'Wow!' said Carl. 'Bet they cost millions. Bet people were desperate to have one.'

'Yes,' said Harrison. 'But he'd only sell them to people who were nice.'

Carl thought for a second and then he said, 'But what if someone horrible got hold of one?'

'Dunno,' said Harrison. 'Maybe he put a spell on it or something.'

'Wow!' said Carl.

'Anyway,' said Harrison. 'When Fred was nearly ninety, he said he'd make one last violin and then retire in time for Christmas. It was going to be the most amazing, fantastic, brilliant violin ever made!'

'I bet everyone wanted it, then,' said Carl.

'They did. People were posting money through Fred's letterbox. They were banging on his windows. They were trying to squeeze down his chimney.'

'Like Santa.'

'Except Santa wouldn't shout, "Give me your violin or else," would he?'

'No,' said Carl. 'He'd say "PLEASE".'

'Anyway, guess who was shouting the loudest?'

Carl shook his head.

'Madame Zara, 'cos her little daughter Mara had put Fred's special violin at the top of her Christmas list.'

'I expect,' said Carl, 'you're going to tell me that little Mara grew up to be *Madame* Mara, famous violin teacher.'

Harrison nodded. 'But Fred didn't like Mara's mum. Zara was bossy and not very nice. So he told her to clear off.'

'Poor Zara.'

'You won't think that when you hear what happened next,' said Harrison. 'She tried to STEAL it.'

'*Tried* to steal it?' said Carl.

'Yep. But she was too late. Fred had given it away.'

'Who to?' asked Carl.

'Can't you guess?' said Harrison.

'No, but *I* can!' said Madame Mara,
appearing suddenly at Harrison's back.

She snatched the violin out of
Harrison's hand. Its strings twanged
horribly.

'And now it's mine,' she cried.

'No, it's not,' said Harrison snatching
it back.

'Yes, it is!'

'No, it's not!'

Madame Mara was pulling one way.
Harrison was pulling the other. Carl was
trying to tread on Madame Mara's feet.
They were making a lot of noise.

'Harrison Bellringer! Carl Westway!'
said Mrs Pauley, striding across to where
they were scrapping. 'What is going on?'

'Madame Mara is trying to steal my violin!' cried Harrison.

Mrs Pauley was suddenly all of a twitter. '*The* Madame Mara?' she asked. 'The famous violin teacher?'

Mrs Pauley looked stern.

'Now, Harrison. We all know Madame Mara would never steal anything.'

'Of course I wouldn't,' said Madame Mara, smiling sweetly. 'I just want to keep the violin safe until this evening.'

'There. You see? Madame Mara is only trying to help.' Mrs Pauley prised the violin out of Harrison's hands. She gave it straight to Madame Mara.

There was nothing Harrison or Carl could do to stop her.

7

Simply magic

'Now look here, sonny.' The sergeant behind the desk at the police station was waggling a finger under Harrison's nose.

'You say a little old lady attacked you in the library and then ran off with your violin? Sounds like a whopper porky-pie to me.'

'But it's the truth!'

'It is,' said Carl. 'And her name's Madame Mara Viola D'Amore.'

'Mmn. That name rings a bell,' said the sergeant.

'It's a very special violin,' said Harrison.

'Special?' said the sergeant, beginning to sound interested.

'Priceless,' said Carl, cunningly.

'In that case, I'll get the lads on to it at once.'

But even with the police looking high and low, there was no trace of Madame Mara or the violin. They'd vanished into thin air.

Harrison's mum was very cross.

'Just when you're going to be a star,' she said. 'Never mind, you'll have to play your school violin tonight, instead. Your talent will still shine through.'

Poor Harrison. He'd forgotten all about that. He looked at Carl in horror.

'But I can't play now.'

'Nerves,' said Mrs Bellringer. 'Every player has them. Once you're out there, in front of all those people, you'll be fine.'

'But Mum! You're not listening. I can only play great grandma's violin.'

'There's chickenpox about,' said Carl. 'Harrison looks a bit pale.'

'Nice try,' whispered Harrison.

But it wasn't any good. He was going to have to stand up at seven that evening and play *Twinkle, Twinkle* on his school violin. It would be heart-stoppingly, gut-wrenchingly horrible. He'd never be able to play the violin again.

Mmn, he thought, cheering up. Not all bad then.

That evening, the school hall was packed. There were reporters, photographers, TV camera crews and all Harrison's teachers.

'Don't worry,' whispered Carl. 'Madame Mara won't turn up. She was only after the violin.'

'But they'll still want me to play,' said Harrison looking very gloomy.

At five past seven, Harrison knew he couldn't hold out any longer. He'd tuned the violin, waxed the bow and coughed a lot. The audience was getting restless. He was going to have to play.

Then, just as he screeched the first note, there was a big kerfuffle at the back of the hall.

It was Madame Mara, in full evening dress and covered in jewels.

'Stop!' she said. 'This boy is useless. Let *me* play.'

In a flash, she'd nipped on stage and pushed Harrison out of the way.

'Now, just a minute,' said Mr Batz.

But Madame Mara wasn't listening. Eyes blazing with excitement, she lifted Fred's violin and tucked it under her chin.

She started to play. She didn't look like an old woman any more. She looked like a young girl dreaming.

The whole room fell silent. Her playing was simply magical.

Then something horrible started to happen.

The violin began to sound harsh and rasping. *Screech. Whine. Shriek.*

The noise was making people cover their ears. Their faces were twisting in pain.

'Stop her!' they were shouting.

Harrison knew that he had to do something. He felt dizzy and sick. So he rushed forward and tried to take the violin off Madame Mara.

'Please,' he was saying. 'You've got to stop. It's not your violin. Fred didn't want you to have it.'

'It should have been mine,' Madame
Mara screeched. 'It was top of my
Christmas list. I've spent my whole life
looking for it. I deserve to have it.'

'But it's no good,' said Harrison.
'You'll never be able to play it. Fred put
a spell on it.'

Madame Mara stopped. 'If I can't play
it, nobody will!' she screamed.

Before Harrison could stop her, she'd thrown the violin to the floor and was jumping all over it.

Splinter. Crash. Twang. Crunch.

Then she leapt from the stage with a wild cackle. She was trying to push her way through the crowd, when a voice called out, 'Stop that woman!'

It was the sergeant from the police station. He was looking very pleased with himself.

'Madame Mara,' he said. 'I thought I knew that name. We had a fax about her last week. She's wanted on five different continents for the theft of valuable violins. There's a reward for her arrest.'

Harrison dived off the stage and made a lunge for Madame Mara. He grabbed at the hem of her dress.

She toppled forward and was neatly caught by the sergeant.

'You're nicked,' he said, clapping her in handcuffs.

It took ages for the fuss to die down.
Harrison had to collect the reward on
television. His picture made the front
page in all the papers and he was
interviewed on the six o'clock news.

'Well, Harrison,' they said. 'The
reward. It's a lot of money. What will
you spend it on? Another violin?'

'No way,' he said. 'I'm never going
near a violin again. No, I'm going to
buy my mum a new car.'

'Are you sure about that?' Mrs
Bellringer kept asking. 'You may still
have hidden talent.'

'Are you sure about that? You can still have lessons,' said Mr Batz on Tuesday lunchtime.

'Quite sure, thank you,' said Harrison.

'Oh good,' said Mr Batz. 'I'm glad you're sure.'

'Oh good,' said Emily Snell.

'Oh great,' said Carl, on Tuesday after school. 'Now you can go back to playing football.'

'And finish your project,' said Mrs Bellringer. 'What was it again?'

'You never listen,' sighed Harrison. 'It's on Egyptian mummies.'

'I made a life size mummy when I was at school,' said Mrs Bellringer. 'There was even a curse on it.'

'What kind of curse?' asked Carl.

'Something about a plague of boils, I think. Bet I've still got it in the attic. Shall I go and look?'

'No thanks,' said Harrison quickly. 'We'll probably make our own.'

About the author

When I was Harrison's
age, I used to play the
violin. I had a great
teacher, but I was lazy.
I never did any practice.
I used to hope that
somehow, magically,
I'd be able to play!

I've still got my violin. I keep it
wrapped up in a silk scarf, in a black
case by the piano. It's very old, but it
isn't at all magical. I know, because
when I started writing this story, I tried
it out and guess what? I made a noise
that sounded just like two cats fighting!